Lee Canter's
Teaching Responsible Homework Habits

Upper Elementary — Grades 4-6

CONTENTS

OVERVIEW	2
SECTION 1: How to Establish a Homework Policy	4
SECTION 2: Teaching Your Students How to Do Homework	7
Lesson 1—Introducing the Homework Policy	9
Lesson 2—Returning Homework to School on Time	11
Lesson 3—Setting Up a Study Area	15
Lesson 4—Creating a Homework Survival Kit	23
Lesson 5—Scheduling Daily Homework Time	29
Lesson 6—Doing Homework on Your Own	35
Lesson 7—Rewarding Yourself for Homework Success	39
Lesson 8—How to Schedule Long-range Projects	43
Follow-Up Awards for Lessons 1-8	49
SECTION 3: How to Motivate Students to Do Their Homework	53
SECTION 4: What to Do If Students Do Not Complete Homework	57
Parent Resource Sheets	60

A Publication of Lee Canter & Associates

TEACHING RESPONSIBLE HOMEWORK HABITS

Homework. It's one of the most frequently recurring problems at school—but it doesn't have to be. This book is dedicated to helping you teach students how to do homework, and do it well.

Every time you give a homework assignment, you are involving three groups of people in the homework process: your students, their parents, and yourself. By following the guidelines presented in the four sections of this book, you'll learn your part in the homework process, how you can get parents to provide support and motivation at home, and just how you can help your students achieve success.

SECTION #1—How to Establish a Homework Policy

Lay the foundation for student success by first developing a homework policy. A homework policy clearly states your expectations for everyone involved in the homework process— and demonstrates to parents and students the importance you place on homework. See pages 4-6 for easy-to-follow guidelines for developing an effective homework policy.

SECTION #2—Teaching Your Students How to Do Homework

Many students have difficulty with homework simply because they lack proper study habits. This section gives you a series of eight lessons that will teach your students—and inform their parents—how to do homework responsibly. The assignments contained in the lessons are designed to be the first homework assignments the students receive during the school year. What your students learn from these beginning-of-the-year lessons can then be applied to homework assignments throughout the rest of the school year.

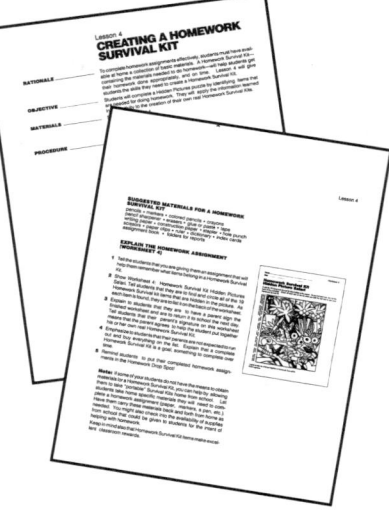

Each lesson contains a comprehensive **Teacher's Lesson Plan** outlining the rationale, objective and procedure for the lesson.

Each lesson contains one or more **Student Worksheets** to reinforce and expand the lesson.

Each lesson contains a **Parent Tip Sheet** designed to keep parents informed of specific ways they can help their child do homework successfully.

Motivate your students to adopt the responsible homework habits taught in the eight lessons by sending home fun-filled follow-up **Awards**—a different one for each lesson!

SECTION #3—How to Motivate Students to Do Their Homework

Once you have taught students how to do homework, you must provide motivation for students to complete homework on a regular basis. This section provides guidelines and reproducibles for reinforcing good homework habits with praise and other positive motivators.

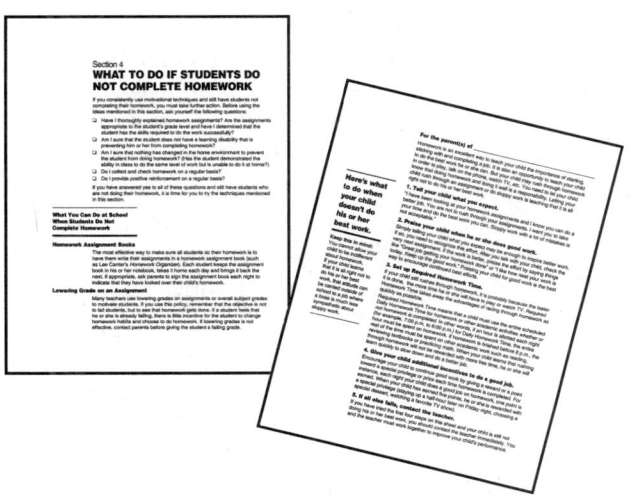

SECTION #4—What to Do If Students Do Not Complete Homework

If you consistently use the motivational ideas in Section 3 and continue to have students who do not complete their homework, you must take further action. Once you have determined that a student is capable of doing the assignments, but is simply choosing **not** to do the work, consider using the techniques on pages 57 - 59 in this section. Reproducible parent resource sheets are also provided for you to give parents to help them solve the most common homework problems.

Teaching Responsible Homework Habits ©Lee Canter & Associates

Section 1
HOW TO ESTABLISH A HOMEWORK POLICY

Teachers who have an effective approach to homework start by developing a **homework policy**. A homework policy is a written homework plan that clearly spells out the type and amount of homework you will give, the manner in which you expect students to do their homework, and the type and degree of support you expect from parents. Your school or district may already have a homework policy in place for you to use. If one is not in place, it is important that you establish one now.

Your homework policy should include the following information:

Give a rationale for homework.

You can't assume that students or parents understand why homework is given or how important it is. Therefore, you should explain the benefits of homework and why you are going to give it. For example, homework reinforces skills and material learned in class, prepares students for upcoming lessons, teaches students to work independently, and helps students develop positive study habits. (See paragraph 1 of the sample Homework Policy, page 6.)

Explain the types of homework you will assign.

It is important that both parents and students know that you are doing your part to ensure that students have the ability to do the homework you assign. Your policy should state that the homework you assign will require only those skills students have already learned in class.

Inform parents of the amount and frequency of homework.

Research has shown that regular homework assignments produce more learning than less consistently assigned homework. It is important, therefore, for your homework policy to include the days of the week on which you will assign homework and the amount of time it should take students to complete homework. (See paragraph 2 of the sample Homework Policy, page 6.)

Provide guidelines for when and how students are to complete homework.

You must clearly define in your policy how you expect students to go about doing their assignments. Typical expectations might include that:

- All assignments will be completed.
- Students will do homework on their own and to the best of their ability.
- Students will turn in work that is neatly done.
- Students will turn in all homework assignments on time.
- Students are responsible for making up homework assignments missed due to absence.

Explain your homework record keeping system.
Your homework policy should state that you will keep a daily record of all homework assignments completed and not completed. This will both motivate students to do their work and show parents and students the value you place on each and every assignment.

Explain how homework will affect students' grades.
Students and parents need to know how homework will be graded. Many schools list homework as a separate item on report cards. Others consider homework as part of a citizenship grade or a subject grade. Whatever system you use should be stated clearly in your homework policy.

Explain how you will positively reinforce students who complete homework.
Your homework policy should state the specific ways you plan to reinforce students when they complete homework—praise, awards, notes to parents, etc.

Detail what you will do when students do not complete their homework.
In some instances students may be prevented from doing homework by circumstances outside of their control. Be sensitive to these situations. For most students, however, it is not that they *can't* do their homework, it is that they *won't* do it. When students choose not to do their homework, you can take actions such as:

- Have parents sign completed homework every night.
- Have students miss recess to complete homework.
- Have students complete homework in after-school detention.
- Lower students' grades.

Homework missed for legitimate reasons must be explained in a signed note from the parents.

Clarify what is expected of parents.
Research has shown that parents are a key factor in children's achievement in school. Parents, therefore, must play an important role in the homework process. Your homework policy needs to cover the specific types of support you expect from parents. You should expect parents to:

- Establish homework as a top priority for their child.
- Make sure that their child does homework in a quiet environment.
- Establish a specific time each day for homework to be completed.
- Provide positive support and encouragement when homework is completed.
- Not allow their child to get out of doing homework.
- Contact you if their child is having problems with homework.

Share your Homework Policy with your administrator, students, and parents.

Once you have developed your plan, present it to your administrator for approval. Then reproduce copies of your policy, distribute to students, and have a discussion regarding the guidelines. A written copy of your homework policy should be sent home to parents, too. Include a letter instructing parents to discuss the policy with their child. Provide a tear-off section on the accompanying letter for parents and student to sign acknowledging that they've read and discussed the homework policy. Have students bring the signed portion back to school.

The following sample demonstrates how to incorporate
all the elements of a homework policy into a one-page reproducible.

Sample Homework Policy

Dear Parents,

I believe homework is important because it is a valuable aid in helping students make the most of their experiences in school. I give homework because it reinforces what has been learned in class, prepares students for upcoming lessons, teaches responsibility and independence, and helps students develop positive study habits.

I will assign homework Monday through Thursday nights. Homework should take no more than one hour to complete each night, not including time spent studying for tests and working on long-range projects. Spelling tests will be given each Friday. Students will be given at least one week's notice to study for all tests. There will be two written reports due this year—one due in January and one due in May.

I expect students to do their best job on all homework assignments. Homework should be neat, not sloppy. I expect students to do homework on their own and only ask for help after giving it their best effort.

I will check all homework assignments. I strongly believe in the value positive support plays in motivating children to develop good study habits. I will give students praise and other motivational incentives when they do their homework.

If a student chooses not to do an assignment, I will ask that parents begin checking and signing completed homework each night. If the student still chooses not to complete homework, he or she will choose to lose certain privileges. If a student chooses to make up incomplete homework assignments the next day, the homework will be accepted but the assignment will receive a one-grade reduction. If a student chooses not to make up a missed assignment, he or she will receive a fifteen-minute detention for each homework assignment missed and parents will be contacted by phone or in writing.

If there is a legitimate reason why a student is unable to finish a homework assignment, the parent must send a note to me on the day the homework is due stating the reason it was not completed. The note must be signed and dated by the parent.

I feel that parents are the key to making homework a positive experience for their children. Therefore, I ask that parents make homework a top priority by providing necessary homework supplies and a quiet environment in which to study. I recommend that parents set aside a specific time each day for homework to be completed. Parents should provide praise and support for all homework efforts, but should not allow children to avoid homework.

Parents should help with homework only after their child has tried his or her best to do the assignment independently. Under no circumstances should parents do homework assignments for their children.

I will be sending home worksheets to help students learn how to develop good homework habits. I will also include Parent Tip Sheets that specify how parents can help in the homework process. Please review the worksheets and tip sheets together.

Teacher's Signature

Section 2
TEACHING YOUR STUDENTS HOW TO DO HOMEWORK

Many students have difficulty with homework simply because they have not been taught how to do homework or do not possess strong study skills. Many students forget to bring assignments back to class, they study in front of TV sets or while talking on the phone, and they always seem to have time in their busy schedules for everything but homework.

This section gives you a series of lessons that will teach your students—and inform their parents—how to do homework responsibly. The assignments contained in the lessons are designed to be the first homework assignments the students receive during the school year. If possible, these lessons should be presented during the first few weeks of school.

To be most effective, these lessons must be presented before any academic homework is assigned.

These are the lessons included in this chapter.

Lesson 1: Introducing the Homework Policy
Lesson 2: Returning Homework to School on Time
Lesson 3: Setting Up a Study Area
Lesson 4: Creating a Homework Survival Kit
Lesson 5: Scheduling Daily Homework Time
Lesson 6: Doing Homework on Your Own
Lesson 7: Rewarding Yourself for Homework Success
Lesson 8: How to Schedule Long-range Projects

Each lesson includes the following components:

● A **Teacher's Lesson Plan** outlining the rationale, objective and procedure for the lesson. The lesson plans are contained within this section.

● **Student Worksheets** to reinforce and expand the lesson. The Student Worksheet reproducible masters follow each lesson plan. (Note: There is no Student Worksheet for Lesson 1.)

● A **Parent Tip Sheet** designed to keep parents informed of specific ways they can help their children do homework successfully. The Parent Tip Sheet for each lesson follows the Student Worksheet(s) for the lesson. (Note: There is no Parent Tip Sheet for Lesson 1)

● A follow-up **Award** is included for each of the eight lessons. These fun-filled awards are given to students after each lesson has been successfully completed.

To use the lessons in this section most effectively, first determine a time frame in which you will teach the lessons.

Note: To be most effective, all the lessons should be taught in sequence during the first few weeks of school.

Follow this sequence when presenting each lesson:

1. Read the lesson plan to familiarize yourself with the rationale, objectives and activities for the lesson.

2. Make one copy for each student of the Student Worksheet(s) and Parent Tip Sheet for the lesson.

3. Teach the lesson to your students:
    - Introduce the concept.
    - Discuss the concept with your students.
    - Explain the homework assignment and distribute Student Worksheets.
    - Distribute and discuss Parent Tip Sheets. Have students take home their worksheets and Parent Tip Sheets.
    - Follow up as indicated on the lesson plan.

4. Hand out follow-up Awards at your discretion.

Note: Each lesson has been organized into a self-contained unit for easy removal, reproduction and storage.

You are now ready to begin teaching your students to do their homework responsibly. Proceed to Lesson 1 on the next page.

Lesson 1
INTRODUCING THE HOMEWORK POLICY

RATIONALE — A homework policy establishes a firm foundation for homework by stating the expectations and responsibilities of everyone involved in the homework process—teacher, students, and parents. In Lesson 1, students will be introduced to your homework policy and learn exactly what is expected of them regarding homework.

OBJECTIVE — After being introduced to the homework policy in class, the students will take home a copy of the policy, discuss it with their parents, obtain appropriate signatures, and return signatures to school.

MATERIALS — Homework Policy, Letter to parents

PROCEDURE — **INTRODUCE THE IMPORTANCE OF EVERYONE—TEACHER, PARENT, AND STUDENT—BEING INVOLVED IN HOMEWORK**

1. Tell students that homework involves more than just the student. Explain that homework is a responsibility that involves the teacher, the students, and their parents.
2. Ask students to tell what they think their own homework responsibilities might be. List their ideas on the board.
   Examples:
   - Remembering to take homework assignments home.
   - Remembering to do the assignment.
   - Remembering to bring homework back to school.
   - Doing the work neatly.
   - Trying to do the homework on your own.
3. Explain to students that during the next few days you will be teaching them some special skills that will help them do their homework assignments more responsibly.
4. Now ask students to talk about what their parents' homework responsibilities might be. List their ideas on the board.
   Examples:
   - Making sure the student has a place to study at home.
   - Reminding the student to do homework.
   - Making sure that necessary homework supplies are available.
   - Helping the student get to the library when necessary.
   - Reading and checking rough drafts.
5. Tell students that it is important for parents, too, to learn about better ways of doing homework—and what they can do to help their children. Explain that during the next few days you will be sending Parent Tip Sheets home that will give their parents lots of information about helping with homework.

Lesson 1

DISCUSS HOW A HOMEWORK POLICY WILL HELP EVERYONE—TEACHER, STUDENT AND PARENTS—UNDERSTAND AND FULFILL THEIR RESPONSIBILITIES

1. Tell students that tonight you are going to give each of them a written homework policy to take home. Explain that a homework policy is a list of standards that will help students and parents understand their homework responsibilities. Read the policy standards to the class.

2. Explain why a homework policy is needed. (So that parents and students alike will clearly understand your expectations about homework.)

3. Tell about the positives you will use when homework is done appropriately. Explain the consequences that will be imposed when homework is not done.

4. Check for student understanding by having them paraphrase each of the standards you read.

5. Give each student a signed (by you) copy of the homework policy and a cover letter to take home to parents.

> Dear Parent,
>
> I believe homework is important because it is a valuable aid in helping students make the most of their experience in school. I give homework because it is useful in reinforcing what has been learned in class, preparing students for upcoming lessons, extending and generalizing concepts, teaching responsibility and helping students develop positive study habits.
>
> I will assign homework Monday through Thursday nights. Homework should take students no more than one hour to complete each night, not including studying for tests and long-range projects. Spelling tests will be given each Friday. I will give students at least one week's notice to study for all tests, and one written report will be assigned each grading period.
>
> I expect students to do their best job on their homework. I expect homework to be neat, not sloppy. I expect students to do the work on their own and only ask for help after they have given it their best effort.
>
> I will check all homework. I strongly believe in the value positive support plays in motivating children to develop good study habits. I will give students praise and other incentives when they do their homework.
>
> If students choose not to do their homework, I will ask that parents begin checking and signing completed homework each night. If students still choose not to complete their homework, they also choose to lose certain privileges. If students choose to make up homework the next day, their homework will be accepted but they will receive a one-grade reduction on that assignment. If they choose not to make up missed assignments, students will receive a fifteen-minute detention for each homework assignment missed. The first time a student receives a detention for missed homework, I will contact the parents.
>
> If there is a legitimate reason why a student is not able to finish homework, the parent must send a note to me on the day the homework is due stating the reason it was not completed. The note must be signed by the parent.
>
> I feel that parents are the key to making homework a positive experience for their children. Therefore, I ask that parents make homework a top priority, provide necessary supplies and a quiet homework environment, set a daily homework time, provide praise and support, not let children avoid homework and contact me if they notice a problem.
>
> Parents should help their children with homework if a problem arises, but only after children have tried their best to solve it on their own. In no case, however, should parents do homework for their children.
>
> I will be sending home lessons to help students learn how to do homework. I ask that students and parents go over these lessons together.
>
> Teacher's Signature

EXPLAIN THE HOMEWORK ASSIGNMENT: TAKE THE HOMEWORK POLICY HOME, READ IT WITH PARENTS, AND RETURN THE SIGNATURE PORTION TO SCHOOL

1. Explain to students that they are to read the homework policy with their parents that night. Tell them that after reading the policy together, you want the students *and* their parents to sign the accompanying letter in the appropriate spaces. (Show the signature portion of the letter.) Explain that their signatures will let you know that parents and students understand what is expected of everyone regarding homework.

2. Tell students that you want them to return the signed tear-off portion of the letter to school the next day.

FOLLOW UP

1. NEXT DAY Collect signed papers. Review the homework policy once more to make certain that all students understand their responsibilities.

2. Put up a charted version of the homework policy in the classroom.

3. Do your part in enforcing the homework policy by always following through with your positives and consequences. Be consistent. Let your students know that in your class homework is important.

Lesson 2
RETURNING HOMEWORK TO SCHOOL ON TIME

RATIONALE — Remembering to bring homework assignments back to school when they are due is an important responsibility a student must develop. Lesson 2 provides students with skills that will help them develop the habit of returning homework to school on time.

OBJECTIVE — Students will choose a spot at home where they will put completed homework assignments each night. They will mark this spot with a "Homework Drop Spot" sign. Consistent use of this Homework Drop Spot will help develop the habit of always putting finished homework in the same place each night—thus making it easier to remember to bring it back to school.

MATERIALS — Student Worksheet 2
Parent Tip Sheet 2

PROCEDURE — **INTRODUCE THE CONCEPT OF REMEMBERING TO BRING HOMEWORK BACK TO SCHOOL EACH DAY**

1 Ask students to think about times they have forgotten to bring homework assignments back to school. Have them give reasons why they forgot (e.g., couldn't find it, were too rushed to remember, lost it).

2 Ask what happens at home on mornings when they can't find their homework. How do they feel? How do their parents feel? How do students feel back in class when they've done the homework assignment and left it at home?

3 Have students brainstorm ideas that might help them remember to bring homework assignments back to school each day.

DISCUSS WAYS OF HELPING STUDENTS REMEMBER TO BRING HOMEWORK BACK TO SCHOOL

1 Tell students that you want to introduce a new idea that will help them bring homework back to school on time.

2 Discuss with students the importance of getting themselves in the habit of putting their completed homework in the same place each night. (Explain that a habit is something that you do so often or for so long that you do it without thinking.) Ask students to share their ideas for special Homework Drop Spots where homework goes as soon as it is completed (Example: Assignment first goes into a notebook, then into a backpack, then in a spot by the front door).

3 Point out to students that if they consistently put homework in the same place each night it will soon become a habit.

EXPLAIN THE HOMEWORK ASSIGNMENT (WORKSHEET 2)

1. Tell students that you are giving them an assignment that will help them remember to bring their homework back to school. Explain that their homework that night will be to complete a Homework Drop Spot word search and to select a Homework Drop Spot at home.

2. Show Worksheet 2: Homework Drop Spot Word Search. Tell students that the words HOMEWORK, DROP, SPOT, and HABIT each appear many times in the word search. Students are to find and circle these words.

3. Tell students that they are to tape the completed word search to the Homework Drop Spot they have chosen at home. Encourage them to use this sign to remind themselves to always put their completed homework in the same place each night. Remind them that consistent use of the Homework Drop Spot will help them develop the habit of always putting homework assignments where they can find them the next morning.

SHOW PARENT TIP SHEET 2

1. Encourage students to compare and talk about what's happening in the cartoons.

2. Explain that the Parent Tip Sheet will give their parents information about helping the students choose a Homework Drop Spot at home.

3. Read the Parent Tips to them as appropriate.

4. Make sure students take the Parent Tip Sheet home.

FOLLOW UP

1. Ask a few students each day to share how their Homework Drop Spots are working so they can evaluate whether they need to make any changes, and so others can hear what works and what doesn't work.

2. Remember that the goal of this activity is to form a habit that the students will benefit from for the rest of the year. Be consistent in rewarding students when they bring homework assignments back on time.

Name _____
Date _____

Worksheet 2

Homework Drop Spot Word Search

Find and circle the words* HOMEWORK, DROP, SPOT, and HABIT in the word search below. The words may appear vertically, horizontally, forward, backward, or diagonally. Good luck!

```
H T I B A H A B I T R S Q V L N
B O R T W O M S H O M E W O R K
U C M I F M G G D R O P S P O T
K L N E O E U R T S H N A T H S
R D T T W W L M C D P F H J A W
O R O I R O D W H I B O M Q B V
W O P B Z R R T M O L L T I I U
E P S A G K O K H L M S P O T H
M N D H I V P S A B H E R R Q A
O T T R B E E P B D R A W Z O B
H M M R O B G O A Z R I B O F I
J K A L U P J T T V M O N I R T
M Z U G G L T A R S S E P A T K
A H O M E W O R K D R O P H L A
I S P O T V T I B A H R T O P S
L R S P O R D K R O W E M O H I
```

*Each word appears 7 times

X marks the Homework Drop Spot!

When you have completed the word search, tape this sheet to the Homework Drop Spot you have chosen. Use the sheet for at least one month to remind you to always put your completed homework in the same place each night.

Teaching Responsible Homework Habits   ©Lee Canter & Associates

Parent Tip Sheet 2
CHOOSE A HOMEWORK DROP SPOT

Remembering to bring homework assignments back to school is an important responsibility your child must develop. Choosing a special Homework Drop Spot at home will help your child develop the habit of always putting completed assignments in the same place each night.

Help your child choose a Homework Drop Spot that's easy to "spot" on the way out the front door in the morning.

PRAISE your child each time completed homework is put in the Homework Drop Spot.

Agree on the Homework Drop Spot your child chooses. Make sure it is in a location that is convenient for you, too.

Respect the Homework Drop Spot. Don't let other things clutter or cover it.

Lesson 3
SETTING UP A STUDY AREA

RATIONALE — Students—and their parents—must understand that to do homework successfully, they must have a place in which to work. The study area must be well-lit, quiet, and have all necessary supplies at hand. Lesson 3 will give students the skills and motivation they need to set up a proper study area at home.

OBJECTIVE — With the help of their parents, students will choose an appropriate study area at home. They will then draw a picture of their personal study area.

MATERIALS — Student Worksheet 3a, Student Worksheet 3b, "Do Not Disturb" sign, Parent Tip Sheet 3

PROCEDURE —

INTRODUCE THE CONCEPT OF DOING HOMEWORK IN A STUDY AREA

1. Have individual students talk about where at home they have done homework assignments in the past. Was this a good place to do homework? What did they like about the location? What, if any, were some of the problems they had working in this location?
2. Share ideas about the following questions:
   Should they do homework in a noisy room? Why or why not?
   Should they do homework in front of a TV? Why or why not?
   Should they do homework while they are eating? Why or why not?
   Should they do homework outside while they are playing? Why or why not?
3. Ask students to brainstorm what a proper study area should be. Make sure that the following points are included: An appropriate study area is one that is well-lit, quiet, and has all necessary supplies at hand.

DISCUSS SETTING UP A PERSONAL STUDY AREA AT HOME

1. Encourage students to share ideas for study area locations in their homes. Ask these students to tell why the location would be a good place for doing homework.
2. Make it clear to students that even if they usually do most of their homework after school in another location (such as the library or an afterschool care program), they still need a place at home where they can study at other times.
3. Emphasize that a study area can be in any part of the home: kitchen, bedroom, living room, den, etc. It doesn't matter where it is as long as it's a place where the student can concentrate and get his or her work done.
4. Discuss the importance of making a personal study area FUN as well as FUNCTIONAL.
   Talk about setting up a study area in such a way that you want to use it—that it suits the way you study.

Lesson 3

- Have the students list on the board all the things they think belong in a study area. Divide the list into two categories:

FUNCTIONAL—Study Area Basics	**FUN—Study Area Extras**
(the necessities)	(the personal touches)
Examples:	Examples:
- Desk or table	- Desk mat of colored poster board
- Chair	- Comfortable, decorative pillows
- Lamp	- Small plant or vase of flowers
- Wastebasket	- Doodle pad
- Supplies (see Lesson 4 on "Creating a Homework Survival Kit")	- Posters or signs
	- Favorite photographs

Note: Recognize that some of your students may have real difficulty finding a quiet place to study at home. They may live in an overcrowded apartment, the environment may be unstable or chaotic, their parents may be unresponsive to their study needs, etc. Help these students explore study area alternatives. Talk about what they can do to help themselves by taking action on their own.

SOME SUGGESTIONS:

1. Find another place to do homework, such as the library or a friend's house.
2. Consistently ask their parents to support their study efforts by keeping sisters and brothers quiet during homework time.
3. Ask parents if one room can be off limits to others in the family during homework time.
4. Arrange with a brother or sister to do homework at the same time.

Be sure to ask students to give suggestions of their own to this problem.

EXPLAIN THE HOMEWORK ASSIGNMENT (WORKSHEETS 3a and 3b)

1. Tell students that, with their parent's help, they are to choose a study area at home. Explain that the homework assignment that night will be to draw a picture of the study area they have chosen.
2. Show Worksheet 3a: My Study Area. Tell students to draw a picture of the study area they have choosen. Point out that the lower part of the worksheet contains spaces for students to write information about their study area. In addition, there is a

space for a parent's signature, and a space for the student's signature. Emphasize that these signatures mean that both parent and student have agreed upon this study area, and that the student agrees to do homework in this location. Instruct students to return the worksheet to school with both signatures.

3 Show Worksheet 3b: Study Area Poster. Encourage students to cut out, color and use this poster to "personalize" their study area. If time allows, let the class brainstorm their own homework phrases and slogans.

SHOW PARENT TIP SHEET 3

1 Encourage students to compare and talk about what's happening in the cartoons.
2 Explain that the Parent Tip Sheet will give their parents information about helping students set up their own study areas.
3 Read the Parent Tips to them as appropriate.
4 Make sure that students take the Parent Tip Sheet home.

FOLLOW UP

1 NEXT DAY Collect Worksheet 3a. Display the returned study area pictures on a classroom bulletin board.
2 Have students color the "Do Not Disturb" sign.
Tell them to hang it in their study area at home.
3 As a related art project, have the students decorate cans or jars to be used as special pencil or pen holders at home. They can also cover various shaped boxes to be used as desktop organizers.

Name _____

Date _____

Worksheet 3a

My Study Area

In the space below, draw a picture of the study area you have chosen at home. Then complete the lower part of this worksheet.

[drawing space]

My study area will be in _____

This will be a good location for studying because _____

_____

I will do my homework in this study area.

Student signature _____

I have agreed upon this study area for my child.

Parent signature _____

18 Teaching Responsible Homework Habits ©Lee Canter & Associates

Name _____
Date _____

Worksheet 3b

Study Area Poster

Color the poster on this page.   Hang it up in your study area.

Teaching Responsible Homework Habits   ©Lee Canter & Associates

Parent Tip Sheet 3
SET UP A STUDY AREA

To do homework successfully, your child must have a place in which to work. The study area must be well-lit, quiet, and have all necessary supplies.

Keep the radio and TV off while homework is being done.

Whenever possible, keep the study area off limits to brothers and sisters during homework time.

PRAISE your child when he or she does homework in the study area.

Help your child choose a location at home in which homework will be done. Even if your child does most homework at another location after school, there still should be a place in the home in which he or she can study.

Remember that your child does not need a lot of space to do homework. The kitchen table or a corner of the living room are fine, as long as they are well-lit and quiet during homework time.

Lesson 4
CREATING A HOMEWORK SURVIVAL KIT

RATIONALE — To complete homework assignments effectively, students must have available at home a collection of basic materials. A Homework Survival Kit—containing the materials needed to do homework—will help students get their homework done appropriately, and on time. Lesson 4 will give students the skills they need to create a Homework Survival Kit.

OBJECTIVE — Students will complete a Hidden Pictures puzzle by identifying items that are needed for doing homework. They will apply the information learned in this activity to the creation of their own real Homework Survival Kits.

MATERIALS — Student Worksheet 4
Parent Tip Sheet 4

PROCEDURE —
INTRODUCE THE CONCEPT OF CREATING A HOMEWORK SURVIVAL KIT

1. Tell students that an important part of getting homework assignments done at night is having all the supplies they need in their study area.
2. Ask students to talk about what happens at home when they can't find something they need in order to complete an assignment. (Example: A report is due the next day and they don't have a folder to put it in.) Share experiences of when *not* having the proper supplies really created a big problem for them or their parents.
3. Tell students that one way to solve this problem is by creating their own Homework Survival Kits. Explain that a Homework Survival Kit is a collection of all the materials they would need to do their homework.

DISCUSS THE KINDS OF MATERIALS THAT SHOULD GO INTO A HOMEWORK SURVIVAL KIT AND DIFFERENT WAYS TO KEEP THESE MATERIALS ORGANIZED

1. Have the students list on the board some of the kinds of materials that should go in a Homework Survival Kit. For each item listed, have students tell how it would help in getting different kinds of homework done.
2. Talk about some of the different ways students can keep all Homework Survival Kit materials in one place at home. Let the students brainstorm types of containers (boxes, drawers, etc.) that could be used.
3. Have samples of some containers available so that students can evaluate the pros and cons of different sizes, shapes, etc. (Is it big enough to hold everything? Is it so deep that things will get lost in the bottom?)

Lesson 4

SUGGESTED MATERIALS FOR A HOMEWORK SURVIVAL KIT

pencils • markers • colored pencils • crayons
pencil sharpener • erasers • glue or paste • tape
writing paper • construction paper • stapler • hole punch
scissors • paper clips • ruler • dictionary • index cards
assignment book • folders for reports

EXPLAIN THE HOMEWORK ASSIGNMENT (WORKSHEET 4)

1. Tell the students that you are giving them an assignment that will help them remember what items belong in a Homework Survival Kit.

2. Show Worksheet 4: Homework Survival Kit Hidden Pictures Safari. Tell students that they are to find and circle all of the 19 Homework Survival kit items that are hidden in the picture. As each item is found, they are to list it on the back of the worksheet.

3. Explain to students that they are to have a parent sign the finished worksheet and are to return it to school the next day. Tell students that their parent's signature on this worksheet means that the parent agrees to help the student put together his or her own real Homework Survival Kit.

4. Emphasize to students that their parents are not expected to run out and buy everything on the list. Explain that a complete Homework Survival Kit is a goal, something to complete over time.

5. Remind students to put their completed homework assignments in the Homework Drop Spot!

Note: If some of your students do not have the means to obtain materials for a Homework Survival Kit, you can help by allowing them to take "portable" Survival Kits home from school. Let students take home specific materials they will need to complete a homework assignment (paper, markers, a pen, etc.). Have them carry these materials back and forth from home as needed. You might also check into the availability of supplies from school that could be given to students for the intent of helping with homework.

Keep in mind also that Homework Survival Kit items make excellent classroom rewards.

Lesson 4

SHOW PARENT TIP SHEET 4

1. Encourage students to compare and talk about what's happening in the cartoons.
2. Explain that the Parent Tip Sheet will give their parents information about helping the students create their own Homework Survival Kits at home.
3. Read the Parent Tips to them as appropriate.
4. Make sure students take home the Parent Tip Sheet.

FOLLOW UP

1. NEXT DAY Collect the signed Hidden Pictures worksheets, check them off, and then return them to the students. Tell them to use the list on the back to keep track of what items they already have at home, and those that they need to add as they begin to create their own Homework Survival Kits. Tell students to check off each item as soon as they put it in their Homework Survival Kit.
2. Encourage students to share the names of local stores where they have been able to find the various materials for their Homework Survival Kits.
3. As a related art project, have the students decorate a small box that they can take home to use in their Homework Survival Kit to keep paper clips, crayons, pencils, etc.

Name _____
Date _____

Worksheet 4

Homework Survival Kit
Hidden Picture Safari

Circle the 19 Homework Survival Kit items hidden in this picture. As you find each one, list it on the back of this worksheet. Check off each item on the list when you add the real one to your own Homework Survival Kit.

Homework Survival Kit items: pencils - markers - colored pencils - crayons - pencil sharpener - erasers - glue or paste - tape - writing paper - construction paper - stapler - hole punch - scissors - paper clips - ruler - dictionary - index cards - assignment book - folders for reports

I agree to help my child put together a Homework Survival Kit.
Parent signature _____

26   Teaching Responsible Homework Habits   ©Lee Canter & Associates

Parent Tip Sheet 4
CREATE A HOMEWORK SURVIVAL KIT

One of the keys to getting homework done is having supplies in one place. A Homework Survival Kit—containing supplies needed to do homework—will prevent your child from being continually distracted by the need to go searching for supplies, and will free you from last-minute trips to the store for folders, paper, tape, etc.

If your child does homework at a location other than home (such as the library or an after-school care program) make sure that his or her homework supplies are available there.

Respect your child's Homework Survival Kit. Don't use these supplies for other family needs.

AGREE with your child that it is his or her responsibility to remind you when any of the Homework Survival Kit materials are getting low and need replacing.

Give Homework Survival Kit materials as gifts. A dictionary, for example, is a special present that a child will use over and over again.

These are the supplies needed for a Homework Survival Kit:
   *pencils ● *pens ● *writing paper ● colored pencils ● crayons ● markers ● ruler ● pencil sharpener ● erasers ● glue or paste ● tape ● construction paper ● hole punch ● stapler ● scissors ● paper clips ● assignment book ● folders for reports ● index cards ● dictionary

*These are the most important supplies your child needs. Try to obtain these items as soon as possible. Add additional homework supplies as you are able to.

You don't need to gather all the materials in one day, but don't wait too long. Your child needs these supplies to do his or her best job on homework.

Teaching Responsible Homework Habits   ©Lee Canter & Associates

Lesson 5
SCHEDULING DAILY HOMEWORK TIME

RATIONALE — Homework—like other activities and responsibilities—must be scheduled into a student's life. Lesson 5 will teach students how to schedule Daily Homework Time that is compatible with personal and family activities, and that also reflects their own best learning styles.

OBJECTIVE — Students will record their daily after-school activities to determine a time each day for homework. They will apply the information learned in this activity to scheduling Daily Homework Time.

MATERIALS — Student Worksheet 5
Parent Tip Sheet 5

PROCEDURE — **INTRODUCE THE CONCEPT OF SCHEDULING DAILY HOMEWORK TIME**

1. Ask students to talk about some of the problems they have had in getting homework done on time. Do they wait until late at night when they are too tired to do a good job? Do their parents "nag" them to get to work? Do other activities and responsibilities (sports, music lessons, babysitting, chores, etc.) ever interfere? Are students usually able to fit these other activities into their schedule? Why do they think that they are able to get to a ballgame (for example) on time, and yet homework is often hastily done at the last minute? The ballgame is scheduled!

2. Tell students that it's important to schedule a Daily Homework Time. Explain that Daily Homework Time is a pre-planned time set aside each day during which they will do their homework. Point out that the purpose of Daily Homework Time is to schedule homework into a student's life, just as other activities are scheduled.

   Note: Be aware of the particular needs of your students. Some students have no structure—or scheduled activites (other than school)—at all in their lives. Emphasize to these students that just as knowing when school starts helps them get to class on time, Daily Homework Time will help them get homework done on time.

3. Ask students to talk about how Daily Homework Time might help them get homework done.

4. Tell students that there are two things to consider when setting up Daily Homework Time: (1) the external time patterns of already scheduled after-school activities and responsibilities (music lessons, sports practice, babysitting, chores etc.) and (2) their internal time patterns that help them know what time of day they function best for doing homework (e.g., right after school vs after a play break).

5. Ask students to name some of the activities that are part of their external time schedules. Do they usually get to these activities on time? Why do they think this is so? Reiterate that these activities are taken care of on time because they are usually scheduled. Homework must also become a scheduled activity.

Lesson 5

DISCUSS PERSONAL TIME PATTERNS

1 Clarify the concept of personal time patterns by doing the following activity in class:

a. Read the Personal Time Statement below:

   I do homework best:
   - right when I get home.
   - after a snack.
   - after dinner.

b. Tell students to go to the left side of the room if the first part of the statement applies to them.

c. Tell students to go to the middle of the room if the second part of the statement applies to them.

d. Tell students to go to the right side of the room if the third part applies to them.

e. After all students have moved to one of the three areas, ask volunteers in each area to explain why that choice reflects their personal time pattern for the given statement.

2 Ask students why they think it's important to take into consideration their personal time patterns when deciding on the best time to do their homework.

EXPLAIN THE HOMEWORK ASSIGNMENT
(Worksheet 5)

1 Tell students that you are giving them an assignment that will help them schedule Daily Homework Time for one week.

2 Show Worksheet 5: Schedule Your Daily Homework Time. Explain to students that they are to fill in all of their scheduled after-school activities and responsibilities in the spaces shown. Point out that by filling in all scheduled activities for a given week, they can clearly see what time is available for homework. Emphasize that students should also think about their personal time patterns. If, for example, Monday afternoon at 4 PM and Monday night at 7 PM are both available for Daily Homework Time, the student should carefully consider which time is best for him or her. Tell students to determine a Daily Homework Time for each day of the week and write it in the spaces shown.

30 Teaching Responsible Homework Habits ©Lee Canter & Associates

SHOW PARENT TIP SHEET 5

1. Encourage students to compare and talk about what's happening in the cartoons.
2. Explain that the Parent Tip Sheet will give their parents information about helping the students schedule Daily Homework Time.
3. Read the Parent Tips to them as appropriate.
4. Make sure students take home the Parent Tip Sheet.

FOLLOW UP

1. **NEXT DAY** Check to see that students have completed their Daily Schedules. Tell them to keep these schedules close at hand, either in their notebook, taped up in their study area, or in some other prominent location such as on the refrigerator. Encourage students to stick to these Daily Homework Times for a week.
2. **ONE WEEK LATER** Ask students to evaluate Daily Homework Time. How many followed their schedules? Did it make a difference?
3. **THROUGHOUT THE YEAR** Make copies of the Daily Schedule (Student Worksheet 5) available for student use.

Name _____

Date _____

Worksheet 5

Schedule Your Daily Homework Time

Do this worksheet with a parent.

Write down all scheduled activities (music lessons, sports practices, etc.) and responsibilities (babysitting your brother or sister, doing chores, etc.) for each day of an average week so you can clearly see what time is available for homework. From the time available each day, think about your personal time patterns and write in the best time for you to do homework each day. Mark your selected Daily Homework Time for Monday, Tuesday, Wednesday, and Thursday in the spaces shown.

Daily Schedule

Monday   HOMEWORK TIME:

3:00 PM _____   7:00 PM _____
4:00 PM _____   8:00 PM _____   _____ to
5:00 PM _____   9:00 PM _____   _____
6:00 PM _____   10:00 PM _____

Tuesday   HOMEWORK TIME:

3:00 PM _____   7:00 PM _____
4:00 PM _____   8:00 PM _____   _____ to
5:00 PM _____   9:00 PM _____   _____
6:00 PM _____   10:00 PM _____

Wednesday   HOMEWORK TIME:

3:00 PM _____   7:00 PM _____
4:00 PM _____   8:00 PM _____   _____ to
5:00 PM _____   9:00 PM _____   _____
6:00 PM _____   10:00 PM _____

Thursday   HOMEWORK TIME:

3:00 PM _____   7:00 PM _____
4:00 PM _____   8:00 PM _____   _____ to
5:00 PM _____   9:00 PM _____   _____
6:00 PM _____   10:00 PM _____

Teaching Responsible Homework Habits   ©Lee Canter & Associates

Parent Tip Sheet 5

SCHEDULE DAILY HOMEWORK TIME

HOMEWORK WITH TEARS

"I'M SORRY DAD, BUT GROWING UP IS A FULL TIME JOB AND I JUST CAN'T FIT HOMEWORK INTO MY SCHEDULE."

Daily Homework Time is a pre-planned time set aside each day during which your child must do homework. During Daily Homework Time all other activities must stop; your child must go to his or her study area and get to work.

Tell your child that homework is to be done during a regularly scheduled Daily Homework Time.

- Help your child determine the length of time needed each day for homework.

- Have your child determine his or her scheduled after-school activities and responsibilities for the week and write them in the designated spaces on the Daily Schedule.

PRAISE your child when homework is completed during Daily Homework Time.

- Encourage your child to identify his or her best personal time patterns for doing homework. (Example: right after school vs. right after dinner)

- Tell your child to determine the best time period each day to be set aside for Daily Homework Time.

HOMEWORK WITHOUT TEARS

"OH HI PAUL, LET ME SEE... I THINK I CAN PENCIL YOU IN AFTER HOMEWORK TOMORROW ABOUT 7PM... BUT PLEASE CALL TO CONFIRM..."

"LET'S SEE... ...SLEEP... ...EAT... ...CHASE CATS... ...SLEEP."

- Have your child write the Daily Homework Times in the spaces shown on the Daily Schedule.

- Check your child's completed Daily Schedule for accuracy. Make sure that the homework times chosen are appropriate.

- Post the Daily Schedule in a prominent location. Encourage your child to stick to the schedule!

Teaching Responsible Homework Habits   ©Lee Canter & Associates

Lesson 6
DOING HOMEWORK ON YOUR OWN

RATIONALE — Doing homework independently teaches a student responsibility and builds confidence and self-esteem. In Lesson 6 students will be encouraged to take pride in doing homework assignments on their own.

OBJECTIVE — Students will use "positive message" acronyms (e.g., W.O.W. —Wonderfully Organized Work) to identify homework assignments they are proud of having done on their own.

MATERIALS — Student Worksheet 6
Parent Tip Sheet 6

PROCEDURE —

INTRODUCE THE CONCEPT OF DOING HOMEWORK ON YOUR OWN

1. Ask individual students to give examples of occasions when they did something on their own for the first time.

   Examples:
   - The first time a two-wheeled bike is ridden solo.
   - The first time a student is paid for a job done outside the family.
   - The first time a student cooks a meal on his or her own.

2. Talk about how they feel when they're able to do something all on their own that they previously needed lots of help doing.

3. Now ask students to share ideas about why it's important to do homework assignments on their own, without a parent's help. Stress the fact that although it may be *easier* to get work done if the student is always asking for—and getting—help, the student will not be learning. Point out that by doing homework on their own, and learning from the assignments, students will do better on classroom assignments, be able to contribute more to class discussions, and will be much more prepared for quizzes and tests. Also emphasize that by doing homework on their own they are learning to be responsible for themselves, and that's something to be very proud of.

DISCUSS WITH STUDENTS DIFFERENT WAYS FOR THEM TO DO MORE OF THEIR HOMEWORK ON THEIR OWN

1. Brainstorm ways for students to do more of their homework assignments on their own.

   Examples:
   - Call a friend if you need help in understanding or doing an assignment.
   - Do the easiest parts of an assignment first so you feel successful. Tackle the hardest parts last.
   - Ask for adult help only when you've tried it on your own and can't go any further.
   - Give yourself positive messages about how proud you'll be when you get the work done. (Example: "I really am a terrific kid!")

Lesson 6

EXPLAIN THE HOMEWORK ASSIGNMENT (WORKSHEET 6)

1. Tell students that you are giving them an assignment that will help them identify work they are proud of having done on their own.

2. Show Worksheet 6: W.O.W. Tell students that each of the squares on this worksheet contains an acronym that is a positive message about a homework assignment. Tell students that they will use the squares to identify homework assignments that they are particularly proud of having done on their own.

   Be sure that students understand that an acronym is a word formed from the initial letters of other words. Here are some examples of well-known acronyms: M.A.D.D. Mothers Against Drunk Driving; N.O.W. National Organization of Women.

3. Read the acronyms on the worksheet to the students:

   W.O.W. Wonderfully Organized Work

   A.C.E. Assignment Creatively Executed

   E.S.P. Extraordinarily Superb Project

4. Point out that there are two blank squares on the worksheet. Tell students that they are to invent a "positive message" acronym of their own for each of these spaces.

5. Tell students that they are to cut out the acronym squares and put them in their Homework Survival Kit. They are also to bring back one of the acronym squares that they have written.

6. Make sure that students understand that the rest of the squares are to be used whenever they wish to identify a homework assignment that they are proud of having done independently.

SHOW PARENT TIP SHEET 6

1. Encourage students to compare and talk about what's happening in the cartoons.
2. Read the Parent Tips to them as appropriate.
3. Make sure students take home the Parent Tip Sheet.

FOLLOW UP

1. Play **Acronym Grab Bag.**
   a. Collect the acronym squares that students have written.
   b. Put these squares into a box.
   c. Ask students to one by one draw a square from the grab bag.
   d. Have a student write the acronym on the board. The rest of the class tries to guess what the initials stand for.

2. Make sure to give students feedback when they have used one of the acronym squares to identify a homework assignment. Make your comments relate to the acronym. (Examples: "You really **ACED** this project." "**WOW!** Great work!")

3. After students have used up their acronym squares, have them mark papers with the acronym itself. Encourage them to keep using this self-reinforcing system throughout the year.

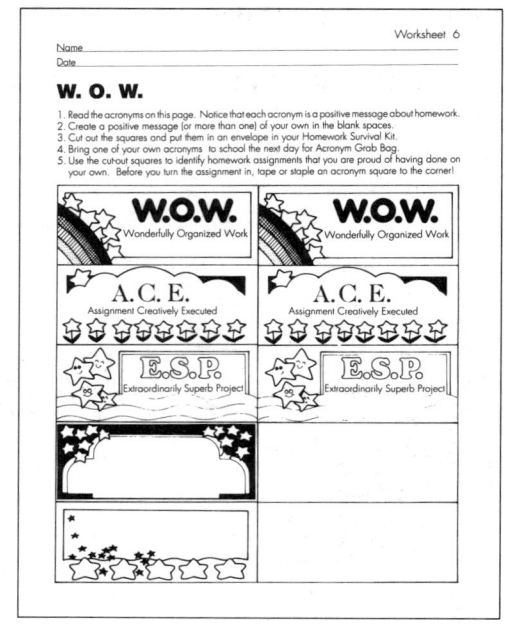

Worksheet 6

Name
Date

W. O. W.

1. Read the acronyms on this page. Notice that each acronym is a positive message about homework.
2. Create a positive message (or more than one) of your own in the blank spaces.
3. Cut out the squares and put them in an envelope in your Homework Survival Kit.
4. Bring one of your own acronyms to school the next day for Acronym Grab Bag.
5. Use the cut-out squares to identify homework assignments that you are proud of having done on your own. Before you turn the assignment in, tape or staple an acronym square to the corner!

Teaching Responsible Homework Habits ©Lee Canter & Associates

Parent Tip Sheet 6
CHILDREN MUST WORK ON THEIR OWN

HOMEWORK WITH TEARS

Homework teaches children responsibility. Through homework, children learn skills they must develop if they are to grow to be independent, motivated, and successful adults: how to follow directions, how to begin and complete a task, and how to manage time. By encouraging your child to work on his or her own, you are helping develop these important life skills.

Check to see that your child is doing homework at the proper time.

PRAISE your child when he or she does homework independently. Let your child know just how proud you really are!

HOMEWORK WITHOUT TEARS

Suggest that your child call a friend if he or she needs help.

Give your child help only if he or she makes a real effort to do the work first.

Lesson 7
REWARDING YOURSELF FOR HOMEWORK SUCCESS

RATIONALE — Praise received from others is a powerful motivator. But students must also learn to take pride in their own efforts and to give themselves a personal "pat on the back" when they are pleased with their work. Lesson 7 teaches students the importance of rewarding oneself for a job well done.

OBJECTIVE — Students will write a list of suggestions of ways that they can reward themselves for meeting their homework goals.

MATERIALS — Student Worksheet 7
Parent Tip Sheet 7

PROCEDURE — **INTRODUCE THE CONCEPT OF REWARDING ONESELF FOR A JOB WELL DONE**

1. Talk about the importance of giving yourself a pat on the back when you've done something you're proud of.
2. Ask students to tell of situations in which they've given themselves a reward for something they've done. Ask them how it felt.
3. Why is it a good idea to reward yourself?

DISCUSS WITH STUDENTS THE CONCEPT OF REWARDING THEMSELVES FOR DOING A GOOD JOB ON HOMEWORK

1. Tell students that it's also a good idea to reward yourself for doing a good job with homework. Ask them to tell about different times they might reward themselves:

   Examples:
   - When I bring homework back on time.
   - When I do my homework on my own.
   - When I keep my Homework Survival Kit filled.
   - When I do my homework without being told to again and again.
   - When I do very neat work.
   - When I do an assignment very creatively.

2. Brainstorm ways students can reward themselves. Make sure the students understand that these must be rewards they have the power to give to themselves. Ask each student to suggest one reward that he or she would be able to give himself or herself.

CONCORDIA COLLEGE LIBRARY
BRONXVILLE, NY 10708

Examples:
- Call a friend when homework is completed.
- Watch a special television show.
- Play a computer game.
- Fix a snack.
- Ride a bike or use a skateboard.
- Play with a friend.
- Have a special dessert.

EXPLAIN THE HOMEWORK ASSIGNMENT (WORKSHEET 7)

1. Tell students that you are giving them an assignment that will help them think about the different ways they can reward themselves for doing a good job.
2. Show Worksheet 7: A Treasure Chest of Rewards! Tell students that they are to "fill the treasure chest" with ideas for rewards they can give themselves. Emphasize once more that these rewards must be things that they really do have the power to give themselves.

SHOW PARENT TIP SHEET 7

1. Encourage students to compare and talk about what's happening in the two cartoons.
2. Read the Parent Tips to them as appropriate.
3. Make sure students take home the Parent Tip Sheet.

FOLLOW UP

1. NEXT DAY Collect and then return completed worksheets to students. Tell them to keep the sheet in their Homework Survival Kit as a reminder of ways to reward themselves when they've done a terrific job on homework!
2. As the year goes on, encourage students to share ways they've rewarded themselves for doing a good job with homework.

Name
Date

Worksheet 7

A Treasure Chest of Rewards!

Fill the treasure chest with ways you can reward *yourself* for meeting your homework goals. Remember, these rewards must be things that you really can give yourself.

Teaching Responsible Homework Habits ©Lee Canter & Associates

Parent Tip Sheet 7
MOTIVATE CHILDREN WITH PRAISE

HOMEWORK WITH TEARS

Children need encouragement and support from the people whose opinions they value the most—their parents. Your consistent praise can encourage your child to feel good about his or her ability *and* motivate your child to do his or her best work.

Each night praise your child about some specific accomplishment. Say something positive about a specific goal your child has set. Example: "I really like how you're doing your homework on your own now."

It is important to PRAISE all homework efforts. Let your child know just how proud you are of how hard he or she is working.

HOMEWORK WITHOUT TEARS

Use Super Praise to motivate your child!

First, one parent praises the child: "I really appreciate how hard you're working to do your homework. You finished it all during Daily Homework Time and you did a great job. I want to make sure Dad hears about this when he gets home."

Second, this parent praises the child in front of the other parent: "Patty did a really fine job on her homework today. She started it without complaining, she stayed with it, and she did a super job on it."

Finally, the other parent praises the child: "I really feel proud of you, getting such a good report from Mom. You're really doing fine!"

If you're a single parent, you can use a grandparent, a neighbor, or a family friend as your partner in delivering Super Praise. Any adult whose approval your children will value can fill the role of the second person offering praise.

Lesson 8
HOW TO SCHEDULE LONG-RANGE PROJECTS

WHEN TO PRESENT THIS LESSON — At the time you give students any long-range assignment such as a written report, book report, or test study.

RATIONALE — Long-range assignments are often the most difficult assignments students are asked to do. This is primarily because students lack the time-management and organizational skills vital to completing the work. Lesson 8 teaches students how to schedule all the steps of a long-range project so that the deadline can be met.

OBJECTIVE — Whenever given a long-range assignment, the students will use the Long-Range Planner to break the assignment into a scheduled series of steps with a "mini-deadline" for each step.

Note: The *process* of learning to do a long-range project is as important to young students as the final project itself. Keep in mind that your goal is for students to succeed. By assigning mini-deadlines for each step of the project, you can more effectively intervene and keep students on track, on time, organized and effectively learning the process of handling a long-range assignment.

MATERIALS — Long-Range Planner
Parent Tip Sheet 8

PROCEDURE — **INTRODUCE THE CONCEPT OF BREAKING A BIG ASSIGNMENT DOWN INTO A SERIES OF LITTLE STEPS**

1 Tell students that they are going to be working on a long-range project. (Describe the specific project: written report, book report, test study, etc.)

2 Have students think back to the last assignment they had of this type. Ask how many students remember feeling overwhelmed by the project or felt a last-minute panic just before it was due.

3 Encourage students to talk about why they might have had these feelings. Examples:
- They didn't plan ahead.
- They waited until the last minute to begin work.
- All the research books were checked out of the library by the time they finally got started.
- There was so much to do they just didn't know where to begin.

4 Tell students that you are going to teach them to plan and organize their project so that they will learn to avoid these problems. Tell them that the key to solving the problems is to break the big assignment down into a lot of little assignments, each with its own deadline.

DISCUSS THE LONG-RANGE ASSIGNMENT THAT YOUR STUDENTS WILL BE DOING

1 Describe the assignment in detail and give its due date.

2 Ask students to think about all the steps they have to do to get this assignment done. List ideas on the board. (Examples for a term paper: do research, check out books, write an outline, take notes, etc.)

3 Point out that, unless they organize all of these steps, it's very easy to get caught at the deadline without work being completed. For that reason, you and they are going to set up a series of mini-deadlines that will help them get the work done on time.

4 Write on the board the steps you have determined are required to complete all parts of this assignment. (Your steps will most likely encompass all of the suggestions given by the students.) Do not write the steps in their proper sequence.

Note: The examples below show a hypothetical series of steps for 3 different long-range projects. These steps may or may not meet the particular requirements of your assignment, and are used only as an example. Determine the sequence of steps you want your students to follow for the long-range project before presenting this lesson.

Examples of Steps for a Written Report
Step 1: Pick out a topic for the report.
Step 2: Do research.
Step 3: Decide what questions you want to answer in the report.
Step 4: Take notes about the topic.
Step 5: Write the rough draft.
Step 6: Write the final draft.

Examples of Steps for a Book Report
Step 1: Choose a book.
Step 2: Read the book; Take notes as you read.
Step 3: Write a rough draft of the book report.
Step 4: Write a final draft of the report.

Examples of Steps for Studying for a Test
Step 1: Organize all test material.
Step 2: Make test study cards.
Step 3: Answer study questions at the end of the chapter.
Step 4: Review all material.

5 As a whole-class activity, have the students sequence these steps in their logical, proper order. Which step would come first? Second? etc. Ask students to explain their reasons for the order. After the class is in agreement, have one student write the final sequenced list on the board.

Lesson 8

EXPLAIN HOW TO USE THE LONG-RANGE PLANNER

1. Hold up a copy of the Long-Range Planner. Tell students that using a Long-Range Planner before they do anything else on the assignment will help them schedule their big, overwhelming project into smaller, more manageable steps. Explain that each of the steps listed on the board will have its own deadline. If they meet all these deadlines, then the final deadline should be no problem!

2. Distribute a copy of the Long-Range Planner to each student.

a. Instruct the students to copy the steps for doing the long-range project from the board. Show them where to write the steps on the Long-Range Planner.

b. Tell students to fill in the final due date on the "Date to Be Completed" space of the last step they filled in.

3. Say to students, "Now let's come up with deadlines for each of the other steps. How long do you think it will take you to complete Step 1?" Share ideas and agree upon a deadline for the first step. Continue in this manner until deadlines have been set for each of the steps. Work back and readjust deadlines as needed, so that everything will be done by the final deadline.

4. Finish the lesson by emphasizing the importance of sticking to these mini-deadlines. Tell the students that you will be checking their progress at each deadline.

5. Tell students to take the Long-Range Planner home that night and go over it with their parents. Point out that next to each "Date to Be Completed" space on the Planner there is a space for a parent's signature. Tell students that you will expect their parents to sign as each mini-deadline is met. The parent's signature will verify that their child has completed the step.

SHOW PARENT TIP SHEET 8

1. Encourage students to compare and talk about what's happening in the cartoons.

2. Explain that the Parent Tip Sheet will give their parents information about how to use the Long-Range Planner.

3. Read the Parent Tips to them as appropriate.

FOLLOW UP

1. Post a schedule of the mini-deadlines in the classroom. Tell students that on these dates you will be checking their work-in-progress. Explain that on these dates you will expect to see their Long-Range Planner signed by parents, and the current status of work done on the project.

2. Follow through by checking students' work at each mini-deadline. Provide plenty of praise and positive reinforcement as students meet these deadlines.

3. Give each student a supply of Long-Range Planners to keep in his or her study area. Encourage them to use the Long-Range Planner for any project that involves many steps and a lengthy period of time in which to complete it.

Teaching Responsible Homework Habits ©Lee Canter & Associates

LONG-RANGE PLANNER

NAME _____ DATE _____

ASSIGNMENT _____ DUE DATE _____

STEP 1
_____
_____

Date to be completed _____

Parent's Initials _____

STEP 2
_____
_____

Date to be completed _____

Parent's Initials _____

STEP 3
_____
_____

Date to be completed _____

Parent's Initials _____

STEP 4
_____
_____

Date to be completed _____

Parent's Initials _____

STEP 5
_____
_____

Date to be completed _____

Parent's Initials _____

STEP 6
_____
_____

Date to be completed _____

Parent's Initials _____

STEP 7
_____
_____

Date to be completed _____

Parent's Initials _____

STEP 8
_____
_____

Date to be completed _____

Parent's Initials _____

Parent Tip Sheet 8
USE A LONG-RANGE PLANNER

Long-range projects, with their due dates sometime in the "distant" future, are usually the most difficult assignments children receive in school. A Long-Range Planner can teach your child how to successfully complete longer projects. By using the Long-Range Planner, your child will learn how to break down a big, overwhelming project into small, easily completed tasks, each with its own "mini-deadline." Your child will also learn how to distribute the assignment over the period of time given for the project.

Assure your child that you will help him or her plan long-range projects in advance, but not at the last minute.

PRAISE your child for each mini-deadline that is met.

Agree with your child that he or she will inform you of all long-range assignments when they are first assigned.

Go over the Long-Range Planner with your child. Talk about the importance of meeting each of the mini-deadlines, so that the final deadline can be handled on time and without panic.

If a mini-deadline arrives and your child has not completed the work, use your full parental authority to insist that it is done immediately.

Reward your child for completing a long-range project on time!

Teaching Responsible Homework Habits © Lee Canter & Associates

Earn 3* units of graduate credit

and increase your skills to become the best teacher you can be!

Choose from 7 courses on the hottest topics in education today!

Motivating Today's Learner™
Motivate students to achieve their full academic potential!

Teaching Students To Get Along™ (Grades K–6)
Stop teasing, bullying and arguing in your classroom!

Strategies For Preventing Conflict And Violence™ (Grades 5–12)
Prevent confrontations, fights and student aggression!

Succeeding With Difficult Students®
Reach students with a history of failure!

How To Get Parents On Your Side®
Turn parents into partners and team up for success!

Assertive Discipline And Beyond®
Spend valuable class time teaching, not disciplining!

The High-Performing Teacher®
A "must" for professionals in high-stress situations.

*semester or 5 quarter hours of graduate credit available, depending upon the accredited university offering the course in your area.

Name

Position/District

Home Address

City/State/Zip

(   )
Home phone

Full satisfaction guaranteed or your money back.

**Questions? Call
1-800-669-9011.
Ask for Charlie.**

CC1045 2/95

Place Stamp Here

Lee Canter & Associates
Attention: Charlie
P.O. Box 2113
Santa Monica, CA 90407-2113

Lesson 1/Follow-up Award

To: _____
Student's name

Thank you for returning the signature section of your homework policy to school.

A great start to a great year. Congratulations!

_____
Teacher's signature

Lesson 2/Follow-up Award

To: _____
Student's name

Where's your Homework Drop Spot?

- ☐ In your backpack?
- ☐ On your desk?
- ☐ By the back door?
- ☐ By the front door?
- ☐ In the kitchen?
- ☐ In your room?

Congratulations for choosing your own Homework Drop Spot!

_____
Teacher's signature

Teaching Responsible Homework Habits ©Lee Canter & Associates

Lesson 3/Follow-up Award

To: _____
Student's name

A personal **Study Area** has:
- ☑ proper lighting,
- ☑ all your homework supplies,
- ☑ a place to write,
- ☑ and YOU doing your homework!

Congratulations on choosing a personal Study Area.

_____
Teacher's signature

Lesson 4/Follow-up Award

To: _____
Student's name

Pencils, paper, glue or paste,
Stapler, crayon, ruler, tape.
Everything you need will fit
into your own personal

Homework Survival Kit.

Great Start!
Homework is easier to complete
when you have a Survival Kit.

_____
Teacher's signature

Lesson 5/Follow-up Award

Make time for homework.

Schedule Daily Homework Time!

Thank you, _____ , for bringing your Daily Schedule back to school. Try to follow this schedule every day.

_____
Teacher's signature

Lesson 6/Follow-up Award

To: _____
Student's name

A.C.E.

Assignment Creatively Executed
... and you did it **on your own!**

Good work. Give yourself a pat on the back.

_____
Teacher's signature

Lesson 7/Follow-up Award

To: _____
Student's name

Give yourself a big hip-hip

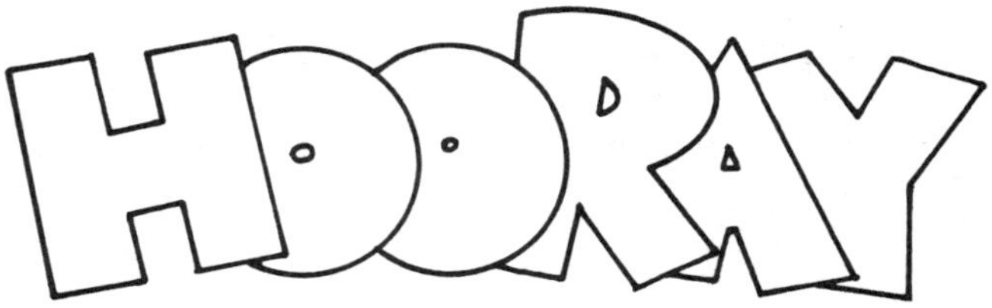

HOORAY

for doing a great job on homework today!

Be sure to reward yourself for your good work.

_____
Teacher's signature

Lesson 8/Follow-up Award

To: _____
Student's name

Thank you for completing your
Long-Range Planner.

Stick to your schedule
and your project
will be
finished on time.

_____
Teacher's signature

Section 3
HOW TO MOTIVATE STUDENTS TO DO THEIR HOMEWORK

For some students, getting good grades may be motivation enough for them to do their homework. But the rest of your students may need something more to motivate them to complete homework.

Positive reinforcement is a powerful tool.
Don't underestimate the power of positive reinforcement. Your positive comments, notes and other incentives could be deciding factors in a student's self-confidence and success in school.

In order to be effective, positive reinforcement must be:
- Something the students like.
- Something you are comfortable using.
- Something you will use on a consistent basis.

Verbal praise is the easiest and best positive reinforcement.
A student who does not do well on homework often has problems in other areas of school. If a student does not feel successful, his or her self-esteem suffers. Your praise can have an enormous effect on a student's self-esteem.

Try these techniques to get the best results from verbal praise:

- **Be specific.** For example, "Mary Ann, this homework paper is very well organized. Your descriptions of life in the old west are very vivid."
- **Be consistent**. Always be on the lookout for praiseworthy behavior and when you see it, give praise.
- **Give positive comments on the content of homework** rather than just the appearance.
- **Praise older students privately** to avoid embarrassing them in front of their peers.

Positive Reinforcement Ideas for Individual Students

A job well done deserves your recognition.
Try these ideas to praise an individual student's homework efforts:

Write positive comments on completed homework.

Positive comments are just the right encouragement many students need to keep up good homework habits. When correcting homework, jot your comments not only at the top of the paper, but throughout the entire assignment. Double your positive message by adding stickers, stamps, or happy faces to your handwritten comments.

Send positive notes home to parents.

Students appreciate notes sent to their parents recognizing that they have done a good job on homework. Also, if parents are fulfilling their role in supporting homework, they will appreciate knowing that their efforts are paying off. It is important that you make positive contact with parents on a regular basis.

When using positive notes to parents:

- Set a goal to send home a certain number of notes per week.
- Be specific with your praise: "Sam has been doing an excellent job getting his homework assignments turned in on time. You should be proud of him."

Chart good homework habits on Homework Cards.

This method of reinforcement allows an individual student to earn points toward a reward or special privilege each time a homework assignment is completed and turned in on time.

Here's how it works:

- Place a homework card on each student's desk.
- Each day that a student completes a homework assignment, place a sticker or write your initials in one of the squares on the card.
- When the entire card is filled, the student earns a reward or special privilege such as extra free time, an award certificate, or class monitor for the day.

Positive Reinforcement Ideas for the Entire Class

Get everyone in your class in the homework spirit! The following ideas are great to get the whole class involved in good homework habits:

Display student homework on special bulletin boards.

Set aside one bulletin board in your classroom to display student homework. Remember to change the homework papers weekly to allow as many students as possible to have their work displayed.

Create a class homework chart.

Make a class homework chart that lists all of the students and provides a place to check every time a homework assignment is turned in on time. When each student has earned 5 checks, the entire class is awarded a special activity (such as a snack or special movie). Using the chart gives you an excellent means of documenting homework completed and not completed.

Conduct a homework raffle.

This reinforcement idea allows all students who complete their homework to have a chance at winning a raffle.

Here how it works:

- The students are told to put their names on both the left and right-hand upper corners of their homework papers.
- When completed homework is turned in, you tear off all the right-hand corners and put them in a jar or box.
- At the end of the week draw a name or two from the jar. The students whose names are drawn win extra free time in class, a tasty treat, or a special privilege.

Positive Notes for Parents

Run off copies of these notes and keep them handy for use throughout the year.

HOMEWORK NEWS FLASH

Dear _____,
Thought you'd like to know that _____ is doing a great job on homework because
_____
_____
_____

Signed _____
Date _____

Dear _____,

HOORAY!

_____
Student's name

did a great job on homework today because _____
_____
_____

Signed _____
Date _____

Teaching Responsible Homework Habits ©Lee Canter & Associates.

Positive Notes for Parents

Run off copies of these notes and keep them handy for use throughout the year.

HOMEWORK SUPERSTAR!

Dear _____,
Thought you'd like to know that _____ is doing a great job on homework because
_____
_____
_____

Signed _____
Date _____

HOMEWORK NEWS

56 Teaching Responsible Homework Habits ©Lee Canter & Associates

Section 4
WHAT TO DO IF STUDENTS DO NOT COMPLETE HOMEWORK

If you consistently use motivational techniques and still have students not completing their homework, you must take further action. Before using the ideas mentioned in this section, ask yourself the following questions:

- ❑ Have I thoroughly explained homework assignments? Are the assignments appropriate to the student's grade level and have I determined that the student has the skills required to do the work successfully?
- ❑ Am I sure that the student does not have a learning disability that is preventing him or her from completing homework?
- ❑ Am I sure that nothing has changed in the home environment to prevent the student from doing homework? (Has the student demonstrated the ability in class to do the same level of work but is unable to do it at home?)
- ❑ Do I collect and check homework on a regular basis?
- ❑ Do I provide positive reinforcement on a regular basis?

If you have answered yes to all of these questions and still have students who are not doing their homework, it is time for you to try the techniques mentioned in this section.

What You Can Do at School When Students Do Not Complete Homework

Homework Assignment Books

The most effective way to make sure all students do their homework is to have them write their assignments in a homework assignment book (such as Lee Canter's *Homework Organizer*). Each student keeps the assignment book in his or her notebook, takes it home each day and brings it back the next. If appropriate, ask parents to sign the assignment book each night to indicate that they have looked over their child's homework.

Lowering Grade on an Assignment

Many teachers use lowering grades on assignments or overall subject grades to motivate students. If you use this policy, remember that the objective is not to fail students, but to see that homework gets done. If a student feels that he or she is already failing, there is little incentive for the student to change homework habits and choose to do homework. If lowering grades is not effective, contact parents before giving the student a failing grade.

Missed Recess or Lunch

A common technique is to have students make up missed homework during recess or lunch. If you use loss of free time to have students make up homework, make sure that:

- Students finish their incomplete work by themselves.
- Talking is not allowed.
- No assistance is given from a teacher or supervisor.

Note: If a student is always spending lunch or recess time doing homework, this may indicate a problem at home that is preventing him or her from working there. If you suspect this, it is time to involve parents.

Study Hall or Detention

Some schools set up homework study halls before or after school that are manned on a rotating basis by teachers.

The guidelines for a study hall or detention room are:

- The room should be supervised by a teacher or other responsible adult.
- No talking should be allowed; this is not a social atmosphere.
- Students must work independently and only do homework.

What Parents Can Do at Home to Solve the Most Common Homework Problems

If problems with homework persist no matter what you do at school, you need more involvement on the part of the parents. All too many parents are at a loss for what to do at home to ensure that their children complete their homework assignments. It is important, therefore, that you supply parents with the knowledge and skills they will need to deal with their children's homework problems. Remember, all parents want their children to succeed. The more you help parents, the more they will be able to help you and their children.

Distribute resource sheets to parents

To help parents deal with their children effectively, we have provided you with resource sheets to give to parents to help them solve of the most common homework problems. These sheets (pages 60-64) give parents step-by-step solutions to most of the homework problems they will face. Parents learn what to do when their:

Child does not do his or her best work on homework assignments 60
Child refuses to do homework assignments 61
Child fails to bring homework assignments or related materials home 62
Child takes all evening to finish homework 63
Child will not do homework if parent is not home 64

Before giving parents any of the resource sheets, make sure that you read them all thoroughly. While each sheet varies slightly, they all more or less give parents these directions for solving their's child's homework problem.

Parent resource sheets state that parents should:

1. Clearly and firmly state expectations to the child.
2. Institute Required Homework Time (as explained on the resource sheets). Determine loss of privileges if child still chooses not to do homework.
3. Provide praise and support for good homework habits.
4. Provide additional incentives for continued good work.
5. Back up their words with action.
6. Contact the teacher if all else fails.

How to Use Parent Resource Sheets

Follow these simple steps for using the Parent Resource Sheets:

1. When there is a homework-related problem you need help with, contact the parents by phone or in a face-to-face meeting.
2. With the parents, discuss the problem their child is having with homework (forgets to bring assignments home, takes all evening to get work done, etc.).
3. Select the appropriate resource sheet and go over each of the steps to make sure the parents understand what is to be done. Then give or send the sheet home to the parents. Don't give the resource sheet to parents if you feel they will be intimidated by it. Just make sure they understand the steps they are to follow.
4. Set a time (in a week or two) to follow up with the parents to determine whether the strategy has been effective or if further action is necessary.

Here's what to do when your child doesn't do his or her best work.

Keep this in mind: You cannot allow your child to be indifferent about homework. If your child learns that it is all right not to do his or her best work, that attitude can be carried outside of school to a job where a boss is much less sympathetic about sloppy work.

For the parent(s) of _____

Homework is an excellent way to teach your child the importance of starting, sticking with and completing a job. It is also an opportunity to teach your child to do the best work he or she can. But your child may rush through homework in order to play, talk on the phone, watch TV, etc. You need to let your child know that doing homework and doing it well is a responsibility. Letting your child rush through an assignment or do sloppy work is teaching that it is all right not to do his or her best work.

1. Tell your child what you expect.

"I have been looking at your homework assignments and I know you can do a better job. You are not to rush through your assignments. I want you to take your time and do the best work you can. Sloppy work with a lot of mistakes is not acceptable."

2. Praise your child when he or she does good work.

Simply telling your child what you expect may be enough to inspire better work. If so, you need to recognize this effort. After you talk with your child, check the very next assignment. If the work is better, praise the effort by saying things like "Great job getting your homework done" or "I like how neat your work is today. Keep up the good work." Praising your child for good work is the best way to encourage continued best efforts.

3. Set up Required Homework Time.

If your child still rushes through homework, it is probably because the faster it is done, the more time he or she will have to play or watch TV. Required Homework Time takes away the advantages of racing through homework as quickly as possible.

Required Homework Time means that a child must use the entire scheduled Daily Homework Time for homework or other academic activities *whether or not homework is completed.* In other words, if an hour is allotted each night (for example, 7:00 p.m. to 8:00 p.m.) for Daily Homework Time, the entire hour must be spent on homework. If homework is finished before 8 p.m., the rest of the time must be spent on other academic work such as reading, reviewing textbooks or practicing math. When your child learns that rushing through homework will not be rewarded with more free time, he or she will learn quickly to slow down and do a better job.

4. Give your child additional incentives to do a good job.

Encourage your child to continue good work by giving a reward or a point toward a special privilege or prize each time homework is completed. For instance, each night your child does a good job on homework, one point is earned. When your child has earned five points, he or she is rewarded with a special privilege (staying up a half-hour later on Friday night, choosing a special dessert, watching a favorite TV show).

5. If all else fails, contact the teacher.

If you have tried the first four steps on this sheet and your child is still not doing his or her best work, you should contact the teacher immediately. You and the teacher must work together to improve your child's performance.

For the parent(s) of _____

Does your child openly refuse to do homework or lie to you or to the teacher about why assignments are not done? When your child would rather battle with you every night rather than do homework, it is time to set firm limits. In order to solve this problem you must make it clear to your child that by choosing not to do homework, he or she is also choosing not to enjoy certain privileges.

Here's what to do when your child refuses to do homework assignments.

Keep This In Mind: Your child must learn that homework is not a battleground. There can be no power struggles over homework; assignments must be completed. Your child must get the message that conflict on this issue will not be tolerated.

1. Tell your child exactly how you expect homework to be completed.

Tell your child, "I expect you to do all of your homework every night. Under no circumstances will I tolerate your refusing to do your homework assignments."

2. Back up your words with actions.

When your child is engaged in a power struggle with you and refuses to do homework, you must make it clear that his or her behavior will result in a loss of privileges. Tell your child, "You can choose either to do your homework or to lose privileges. If you choose not to do your homework, then you choose not to watch television or listen to music or use the telephone until the homework is finished. You will sit here until all of your homework is done. The choice is yours." Then you must stick to your words. It may take your child several days of sitting idly in his or her study area to realize that you mean business and that you won't back down.

3. Praise your child when homework is done.

Praise your child each time he or she does homework. "You've been really responsible in getting your homework done. That's what I expect from you."

4. Use a Homework Contract to provide additional incentives.

A Homework Contract is an effective way to motivate children of any age. It is an especially valuable tool because it encourages a child to accept responsibility for an agreement made between the child and parent. A Homework Contract is an agreement between you and your child that states: "When you do your homework, you will earn a reward." For example, "Each day that you bring home your homework and complete it during Daily Homework Time, you will earn one point. When you have earned five points, you may choose one weekend night to stay up late." The younger the child, the more quickly he or she should be able to earn the reward.

5. If all else fails, contact the teacher.

With a very difficult child, you will need to contact the teacher and arrange for additional disciplinary consequences (such as staying in at recess or after-school detention) to be provided at school when homework assignments are not completed. Your child will quickly learn that school is backing up your efforts.

For the parent(s) of _____

From time to time your child may forget to bring home books or homework assignments. But when your child continually fails to bring home assigned homework or the books and materials with which to complete assignments, then you must take action.

Here's what to do when your child fails to bring homework assignments or related materials home.

Keep This In Mind: Your child must learn to bring home and complete all homework assignments. Accept no excuses.

1. Tell your child that you expect all homework assignments and materials to be brought home.

Tell your child, "I expect you to bring home all your assigned work and all the books and materials you need to complete your assignments. If you finish your homework at school, I expect you to bring it home so that I can see it."

2. Have the teacher send you daily updates on assigned homework.

Ask the teacher to have your child make a list of each day's homework assignments. The list should be reviewed and signed by the teacher and then brought home by your child. After your child has completed the assignments and you have reviewed the completed work, sign the list and have your child return the list and the homework to the teacher the next day.

3. Give your child praise and support when all homework assignments and related materials are brought home.

Make sure that your child knows that you appreciate it every time he or she brings home all homework assignments. "It's great to see you remembering to bring home all of your homework assignments. I knew you could do it."

4. Set up Required Homework Time.

If your child still fails to bring home assignments, he or she may be avoiding homework time to play or watch TV. Required Homework Time takes away the advantages of forgetting homework. Required Homework Time means that a child must use the entire scheduled Daily Homework Time for homework or other academic activities whether homework is brought home or not. If an hour is allotted each night (7:00 p.m. to 8:00 p.m.) for homework, then the entire hour must be spent on homework. If homework papers or the books and materials to complete assignments are not brought home, the entire time must be spent on other academic work such as reading, reviewing textbooks or practicing math. When your child learns that forgotten homework means no free time, he or she will soon remember to bring assignments and materials home.

5. Use a Homework Contract to provide additional incentives.

A Homework Contract is an agreement between you and your child that states: "When you do your homework, you will earn a reward." For example, "Each day that you bring home your homework and complete it during Daily Homework Time, you will earn one point. When you have earned five points, you may choose one weekend night to stay up late." The younger the child, the more quickly he or she should be able to earn the reward.

6. If all else fails, work with the teacher to follow through at school when homework is not completed.

If your child continues to forget homework, phone or meet with the teacher to discuss appropriate follow through at school. By losing recess or remaining after school for detention, your child receives a strong message: Both teacher and parent will work together to ensure that homework is completed.

For the parent(s) of _____

Some children spend hours and hours on homework, when this investment of time is really unnecessary. They may start an assignment, get distracted or begin daydreaming, and then stop doing the work. When your child spends an entire evening doing homework, you need to step in and help

Here's what to do when your child takes all evening to finish homework assignments.

Keep This In Mind: Your child must learn to do homework responsibly and that there are limits to the help he or she can expect from you. Your child must learn to do homework efficiently, productively and on time.

1. Tell your child that you expect all homework to be done during Daily Homework Time.

Tell your child, "I expect you to to get all of your homework completed during Daily Homework Time. Your taking all evening to do homework must stop at once."

2. Make sure that homework is being done in a quiet study area.

Your child may take too much time on homework because he or she is working in a distracting environment. Make sure that during Daily Homework Time your child has no access to TV, the stereo, or other distractions and is not disturbed by brothers and sisters. If such distractions are present now, change the location of the study area immediately.

3. Give your child praise and support when homework is completed on time.

Show your approval by praising your child whenever homework is completed during the designated Daily Homework Time. Give your child encouragement by saying, "Great job! I'm really pleased to see that you completed your homework on time. I'm very proud of you."

4. Provide additional incentives to motivate your child.

Your child may require additional help to develop of the habit of completing homework promptly. The "Beat the Clock" game is an excellent way to motivate your child to complete homework during Daily Homework Time. First, review your child's assignment to determine the amount of time it should take your child to complete the homework. At the start of Daily Homework Time, set a timer (alarm clock, oven timer) to ring at the time you have determined that the homework should be completed. If the child finishes the assignment appropriately within the given time, he or she earns a special privilege.

5. Back up your words with actions.

If you follow the first four steps on this page and your child is still not completing assignments during Daily Homework Time, you must take a stand. Tell your child: "You have a choice. You can complete your homework during Daily Homework Time or you can choose to lose privileges. If you choose not to complete your homework during the allotted time, you will not be allowed to leave the house or visit with friends. You will not be allowed to watch TV, listen to music, or use the telephone. You will sit at this table until your homework is finished. The choice is yours."

Here's what to do when your child refuses to do homework when you are not home.

Keep This In Mind: Your child must learn to bring home and complete all homework assignments. Accept no excuses.

For the parent(s) of _____

If your child refuses to do homework unless a parent is home, you must take steps to help your child develop a more responsible approach to homework.

1. Tell your child that you expect homework to be completed whether or not you are at home.
Tell your child, "I expect you to get all of your homework completed every night, whether or not I am at home."

2. Discuss Daily Homework Time with your child's caregiver.
Inform your child's caregiver of your homework expectations: where your child is expected to do homework (in the study area), when homework is to be done (during Daily Homework Time—which should be posted), and how your child is to do it (on his or her own). Sit down with both parties and discuss this important information.

3. Monitor your child's homework progress when you are away from home.
Telephone your child at the beginning of Daily Homework Time to be sure that homework has begun. If possible, call back at the end of Daily Homework Time to ensure that homework has been completed. Instruct your child to leave all completed homework out for you to check when you get home. Phase out the monitoring process as your child begins to work responsibly.

4. Give praise and positive support.
When you call at the start of Daily Homework Time and find your child on task, say: "I'm pleased that you've started your homework so promptly, even without my being there." When you return home and find homework completed, say: "Great job! I like the way you're working independently while I'm gone. That's very responsible behavior."

5. Use additional incentives when appropriate.
A Homework Contract is an effective way to motivate your child to do homework without your supervision. A Homework Contract should include this information:

- Homework will be done whether or not the parent is at home.
- The amount of time in which homework is to be completed.
- The point system used to reward a child when homework is completed.
- The reward the child will received when a predetermined number of points is earned.

6. Back up your words with actions.
If the first five steps don't help your child complete homework during your absence, explain that all other privileges will be taken away (TV, music, phone) until homework is completed. Let your child know that the choice not to do assignments is his or hers, but that consequences will be given when homework is not done. **Note:** If no one is providing child care, you may have to impose back-up disciplinary consequences as soon as you get home. If you find that homework has not been completed, turn off the TV, get your child off the phone and make sure he or she gets back to work.

7. If all else fails, contact the teacher.
If your child still doesn't do his or her homework, discuss consequences that the teacher can impose at school (recess, after-school detention, etc.).